LIGHTNING STRIKES

Reflections on complicated family relationships

by BONNIE L. BAIRD

LIGHTNING STRIKES
Copyright © 2016 Bonnie Baird
Published by Bonnie Baird
Cover Art Design © Croco Designs
All rights reserved.

ISBN 978-0-9940973-8-5 (print book)
ISBN 978-0-9940973-9-2 (electronic book)

SELECT TITLES ALSO BY BONNIE L. BAIRD

Poetry

WALK ME TO THE DOOR, LOVE:
Notes Written to the Beloved in the First Two Years of Grief

I SMELL STARS:
Final Twelve Years of a Marriage

CLOSE TO THE UNDERTOW:
On the Practice of Ministry

Prose

SURVIVAL OF THE DANGLY GREEN PARROT EARRINGS

CD

WALK ME TO THE DOOR, LOVE

I SMELL STARS

ACKNOWLEDGEMENTS

My deep appreciation to Heather Veinotte, my friend whose writing continues to inspire, and whose support in this craft of writing is invaluable.

Dedicated to my complicated, flawed, and beautiful family (past and present).

CONTENTS

By Marriage

Lightning Strikes

The church is packed and family sits close—
the ones that are and the ones that aren't—
and his darkening face
refusing to acknowledge my question or presence
is like a storm cloud
forming

forecasts were made
and it seems they were accurate:
the air is filling with flashes
of forked energy

no sense trying to get something off the ground in unsettled weather

best sit tight, wait for the strikes to abate

THE LOST ART OF IRONING

The first time he brought me home to meet you
you were ironing
board stretched across the living room
stacks of clothing everywhere
I learned you iron everything
towels
underwear
sheets (even the fitted ones)
easing the wrinkles out with infinite care
I still have the board you gave me,
tired of mattress printed shirts,
though I seldom use it
I've grown accustomed to wrinkles
and who has the time?
still, it's nice when you visit
set up the board
make it all smooth
in the heat

AUTUMN LEAVES

Would that I could let you go
autumn leaves
browned and curled and waiting for the wind

despite sap ebbing
the coming cold
I hold on tight
a tree that will not bare

It's a long way we've come to be together again several months into this new life for you and for us. But then, Thanksgiving is supposed to be about families gathering, isn't it?

Autumn leaves hover on a thin updraft at our feet, their damp smell in the air as we walk up to the front doors. Some sweep in as the plate glass doors slide open. We finally find your room, made familiar with family pictures, Bible, a favorite throw. And you dressed up for the outing. You always did like getting out for drives, for tea.

at night when the lights dim do they shut your door
or can anyone wander in
from another room
another time?

You show us your seat in the dining room, complete with sheepskin throw, stool for your feet. It's bright here and clean and oddly cluttered with people. You introduce us to some of the residents you eat with every day. Elsie who lived on the apple farm down the road from you. Worked hard all her life, widowed for half of it. Louise who went to the same church where you taught Sunday School for years. Few of those you introduce us to can respond in ways we understand. We rely on you to provide background.

*the word **trapped** surfaces*
there's a code to get out
do you know it?
chairs housing bodies that cannot respond
bodies housing minds
of another place
Where will we be someday
when need outweighs ability?

The staff we've meet are patient and kind and call you **sweet** and **dear**. I wonder if they suspect your complexity.

The coal black hair you wore at 10 poker straight
the children you bore from 18 to 39
two husbands and two widowhoods and single parenting in between
the hands that tended livestock
packaged up produce for cityfolk Saturdays at market
cleaned bathrooms and floors
to make ends meet
It doesn't matter anymore
tuck your difference into the closet with your clothes

"This is my son," you say, introducing him to some of your resident friends and staff. "Doesn't he look like his dad!" one woman with good memory and deep roots in the community says.

What was he like, your husband,
at your son's age?
I know him only from photos
and his son's heart
and would he have come here to break you out as he did once
from mother's allowance and singlehood
and do you still miss him this time of year
when leaves swirl and winter's a breath away?

Did you suspect it would be like this when you asked if you could stay with us, that last night when all your things were packed and everything was set but your heart? You never liked institutions. You had good reason not to. Though things are different today.

"He was so little
and they were so big
and even Christmas mornings you had to be careful.
He spent more time locked in closets
and I took most of the beatings for him.
It was seven years but she finally came through.
It wasn't done then, you know, being single and raising
children but she couldn't face seeing us like that
and her knowing how he had just dumped us there
her own brother and us his children.
She knew, like I did,
how to treat family."

I try sometimes to put myself in your place but I can't. Eighty-something is not a time when most would have started a new life. But you did. Sold your home. Moved across the country. Went back to church. Got to know your youngest grandchild, got to know us better perhaps than any of your other family. Forged friendships through it all. Would I have had such courage?

as you turned the key in the lock for the last time
you wondered if you weren't making the biggest mistake of your life
you had, after all,
lived on this piece of land most of your life
your roots were here
they went deep into the soil of this place
like the roots of the trees that afforded a measure of privacy on one side of your
property
how long had you worked the soil of this place?
you recalled the stillness that came from being that close to the land
the smell of it on rainy mornings
you remembered your little daughter
now a senior too
playing among the rows of corn
the graves of two husbands others would have to tend now
it was time to go
to plant yourself somewhere else

still, you thought,
soil is soil

So many boundaries crossed in our time together. We shared a kitchen, a house, a church, two men we both loved. I would never call you **sweet** or **dear** and you would return the favor. Two women from different eras. Yours almost a generation and a half before mine. You ironed everything and I bought wrinkle-free sheets. You needed to know about your family's comings and goings, salaries, dreams, and state of health. I valued privacy. So many boundaries crossed. Did it really matter that much? You worried about little things all the time and handled the big ones with grace.

remarkable
remove a breast and send her home the same day
no exceptions even for octogenarians
in our time with our budgets
the family's got to pitch in
remarkable
that no daughter came
to help or visit
remarkable
a wound so deep
healing so fast
though sometimes it still
weeps

Your voice is so low we can barely hear it and you still have stories to tell. Usually about Allan because it's us you're talking to. How he walked for miles home one night in a snowstorm so your children wouldn't be alone and afraid. How embarrassed one daughter was when you got pregnant with your last child, his first. How excited he was to be a dad.
Did he love you more than your first husband or just differently? And does that explain why your blended family never blended all that well?

over coffee cups we gather
four generations in a little room
the toddlers are playing
and two want one toy and one shoved and the other fell

and one's decorated for something special
and who cares who started it
and the noise is rising and the coffee's on
and did you notice your sister
hugged you and didn't me and why do you suppose she came
and nothing's here but
old grounds dregs of yesterday
an old woman smiling because we're all here
together again

My own mom was excited when she married into a large family. She imagined it would be so much closer than the small one she had come from. I did too. When you die will the link be broken with all of them? It's been stretched to the limit at times over the years and now over your being here and not with us. Maybe it never was that strong to begin with. We are all so different, each of us seeking our own dispensation.

Jacob
demanded a blessing before crossing a river and meeting
his brother foe
demanded of angels
what his own heart couldn't give him
steal a blessing or a birthright and who knows what will haunt you

would it have hurt
to give each child a blessing
the older as well as the younger?
all this wrestling
with each other and ourselves
we might have avoided

The leaves on the hills are turning. We can see them now from the car and this time out for us, for you, is good. Amid the falling leaves, along this stretch of road winding upward into the hills, the colors, I want to ask you something: *As your children by blood and marriage, did we do ok?*

SHELLS

In the morning we find the shells scattered across the deck
torn apart by some night creature

cracked open, sucked dry and flung everywhere, slippery and smelly

when we feast by firelight steeped in wine and memory
something always watches
from the edge

BLACK SHEEP

So who is it in your family? the clergy asks me
just outside the visitation room
confident
I can get the distance well enough to see
for I am clergy too

so much confidence, so little justified

in a family of five siblings and five married-ins
there's always one, sometimes two
pile the grievances on one by one
and send it out into the desert
the black sheep
or was that a goat? there's always one sometimes two
decades now the ritual's been repeating
the gathering together and the piling on and the sending out
for the sake of the rest

And who do you think it is? I ask

Not the one I would name
optics are different if you can get the distance

but that different?

Puzzling

In the wake of three glasses of wine
we offer our pieces of the puzzle that was you

our loves are working from the center out
piling
and sorting
and following connections
and we're on the edges still
after decades and six years past your leaving

and she has a piece that doesn't fit
and my colors are wrong, she says,
we've lost the picture to work from
and who knows how many pieces there actually are

but bordered or centered
patience will count
and coming to the table in pieces for the fitting together
all that matters

GPS

You thrust an old GPS into my hand for the rest of my journey
crucial to get my bearings, right?

no meeting of eyes or acknowledging of what is happening
here between us
just a veering off down some lonesome road

forty years past the point we first met
and I'm still trying to connect

though the point of intersection is past now

BY BIRTH

RELIEVED

I was relieved when he died
though I told no one
and after a few months
dreaming of him hidden
in a spot only he and I knew about
thinking I saw him on sidewalks
always with his back to me
he left me alone
till now
twenty years later with a child of my own
I dream of graves filled with water
bodies that rise
sit at my table
relieved to have surfaced
at last

CLOSE COFFINS

It was a fine piece of wood
warm
and full grained as the man within
lovingly shaped
in a carpenter's hands

hers was small
satin and rose
a chrysalis
hung
between
two poles

PERIOD

Began
the morning the call came

two weeks early

as though it never would
stop

taboo river coursing
generations
mother daughter
daughter mother

beginning again
the morning you died
period

MOTHERBIRD

She would have liked this
you say, looking out over the water
from your treed deck

we watch your daughter try new waterwings

I want to say
I miss her too
our motherlink
body and blood

did you hear motherbird calling
first light?
the nest we watched last night
is empty now
I found
one
feather
on the deck
do you think they're ok?
that she knows?

FIRST MOTHER'S DAY WITHOUT YOU

The affinity to cat
was obvious
early
(insert photo of you at two
clutching your-size cat)

and later
(insert me curled rigid in bed)

when you bridged
the gap
with one padded touch

LAST DAYS OF WINTER

In the last days of winter
the old ones sleep
collapse slowly
into their centers
till nothing remains
but veins meandering towards open sea

Afraid

Lying on this narrow cot beside your bed
I'm afraid to close my eyes

your breathing is ragged
I keep listening for it
to stop

afraid to fall asleep lest I wake with you or your ghost
standing over me
screaming *Get the hell out!*

do you know I am here?
do you mind?

the parcels I sent you
stack in your basement still wrapped
neatly labelled Return to Sender
you always could hold a grudge

how can such a tiny person
contain such large anger?

and is it ok that I'm here
tonight
in this room?

afraid lest you wake
afraid that you won't

Is This Grief Too?

So: is this grief too?
this gaping hole where you used to be
this ragged edge

the photo torn out
or torn down the middle
all evidence of me simply not there anymore

the parcels sent still wrapped and waiting for discovery after you're gone
…return to sender with a skeletal jab

with demise I could at least bury the body, place flowers on top
ask forgiveness of the elements if not of you
convince myself that you somehow know and being in a better place
(perhaps)
find no further room for anger
but this awful silence

when words could lift so much
whispers to the heart: *You are not worth considering*

How do I move past that?

NEXT GENERATIONS

Your Wedding Gift

Your gift was the last one given
at the end of a day of white and red roses
wine flowing like rivers
keepsake photos and cookies made by grandma
exquisite food laid down course by course on white linen

given at the end of a circling of family and friends and two cultures
around a dancing couple

unwrapping by itself from the inside out

spraying the room
transfixing the heart
freezing for all time one awful moment

we might have expected the uninvited guest
to leave such a gift

we've heard fairytales of such things
but this one was Biblical
delivered with a kiss

blood on the wedding pillows
deliberate

NOW THAT IS AN APOLOGY

No Buts immediately following
excusing what was done
how could there ever be an excuse for that?
no expectation of mercy
masquerading as sorrow
or of relationship like it was before

just a straight looking at
full in the face
all the ugliness, the wounding seen and named and owned
though can we ever know fully what we have done?

the beauty of the Other
considered, held up
reflected back

only the Other who matters
only the Other

Inheritance

And you, my son, will get
a double portion
of the family inheritance

from one generation to another
we've passed it along for at least two centuries
something in the blood and in the attitude

manage it as best you can

Grandson's First Day At School

Last night his dad wrote him a letter
capturing feelings so they wouldn't leak out everywhere
simply
disappear with time

So much erased by time
like a great chalkboard
wiped clean except for residual dust, a few missed letters

like the letter we might have written to his dad, to one another
so we wouldn't forget
the letting go and the heart enlarging with possibility and fear
and terrific pride

STONE

This stone has been here for 60 years

lichen and weather have done their part
who lies here is fading

someday memory of this marker will be gone as well
though every generation has its historian
keeper of the secret tombs

who were they really?

this cussedness that runs like a vein through all their namesakes
did they bequeath it to us

and who then to them?
what lies in us because of them?

weather and time
shifting this stone
back to the elements

essence and bone
to all appearances
fading

and yet we're here

In Conclusion

ONE WORD

On my tombstone write one word
not my name
which is three and not that unusual
or arrival and departure dates
which aren't words but numbers
for who on earth (or in earth for that matter)
wants to be a number

one word
for the past
which can't be redeemed without it
one word
for the future which depends on it
one word
for the present, the gift we are given

one word
which I have not been that good at
though I have known those who were and been blessed
write only this:
Forgive

ABOUT THE AUTHOR

Bonnie Baird is a mom and grandma, a writer and an Anglican priest
living and working along the South Shore of Nova Scotia.
She lives with a very bright Siamese cat named Cleo.

www.ingramcontent.com/pod-product-compliance
Lightning Source LLC
Chambersburg PA
CBHW020520030426
42337CB00011B/489